Alfred's Basic Piano Library

# Prep Course

## FOR THE YOUNG BEGINNER

## Lesson Book • Level D

**Willard A. Palmer • Morton Manus • Amanda Vick Lethco**

Cover illustration and interior art by Christine Finn

A General MIDI disk (5719) and a Compact Disc (17162) are available,
which include a full piano recording and background accompaniment.

# Note to Parents and Teachers

The study of music builds character and enriches lives. From the opposite ends of the spectrum, the development of self-discipline and the enhancement of self-expression, music is a beneficial activity for young people, especially in these times when young people need more training in social values. Improved coordination, the ability to work well with others, a sense of accomplishment, an understanding of artistic endeavor, and the appreciation of sensitive interpretation of one of the most noble of the arts, are just a few of the benefits to be derived from music study.

Students who learn to read music well and to perform with reasonably well-developed technical facility will have acquired skills that will bring enjoyment to themselves and to others for the rest of their lives.

PREP COURSE LESSON BOOK D is designed to build on the concepts introduced in Levels A, B & C. It introduces material that will move the students along toward the realization of the ideals mentioned above. This material continues to concentrate on intervallic reading, introducing new concepts that will enable the student to move freely over the keyboard, read fluently in all positions, and develop technical facility equally in both hands.

After a careful review of G POSITION, a NEW G POSITION is introduced, with the left hand an octave higher. After several appealing pieces using this new position, the student is introduced to pieces that change positions during the course of one piece. This is continued throughout the book. The student is drilled in recognizing patterns and playing these figures in any position.

The damper pedal is introduced, and is included in pieces that continue to emphasize hand position changes and fluency in moving over the keyboard.

After a review of sharps and flats and the introduction of the natural sign, the major scale is introduced through the study of tetrachords. Several pieces based entirely on tetrachords serve to reinforce this concept.

In the final pages of the book, pieces are used that combine positions; that is, they have the left hand in one position and the right hand in another. All rhythmic concepts are constantly reviewed and reinforced throughout the book, with strong emphasis on various combinations of eighth-note rhythms.

The book ends with a review of all musical terms studied in Levels A, B, C & D, and the student is now ready to proceed to either PREP COURSE Level E or to ALFRED'S BASIC PIANO LIBRARY, Level 2.

# Outline of Basic Concepts in Prep Book D

# Contents

# The Magic Man

**Mysteriously**

1. Who can pull a rab - bit out of
2. Who can van - ish an - y - thing and

You are now ready to begin Prep THEORY, SOLO, and ACTIVITY & EAR TRAINING BOOKS, Level D.

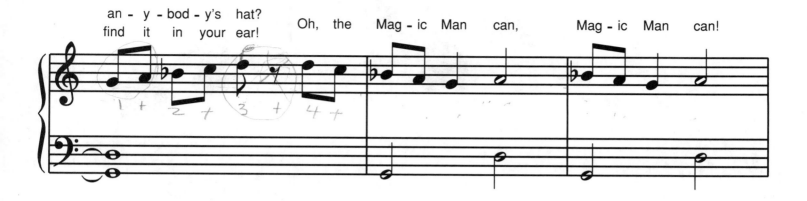

an - y - bod - y's hat? / find it in your ear! Oh, the Mag - ic Man can, Mag - ic Man can!

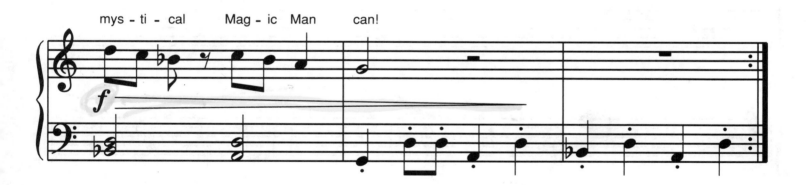

Who can wave a wand and change a mouse in - to a cat? / E - ven take an el - e - phant and make it dis - ap - pear? Oh, the mar - vel - ous, mag - i - cal

mys - ti - cal Mag - ic Man can!

# *Whoopee Ti-Yi-Yo*

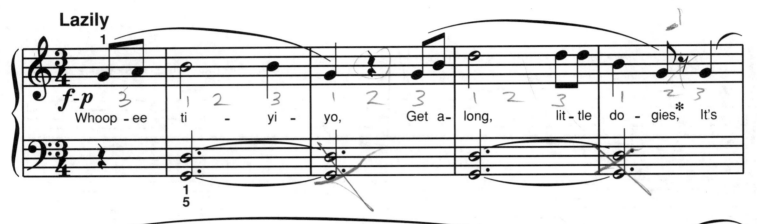

**Lazily**

*f-p*

Whoop - ee ti - yi - yo, Get a - long, lit - tle do - gies,* It's

your mis - for - tune and none of my own; Whoop - ee

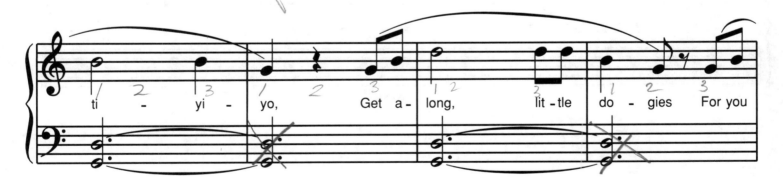

ti - yi - yo, Get a - long, lit - tle do - gies For you

know Wy - om - ing will be your new home!

*A dogie is an orphaned calf.

# Rock It Away!

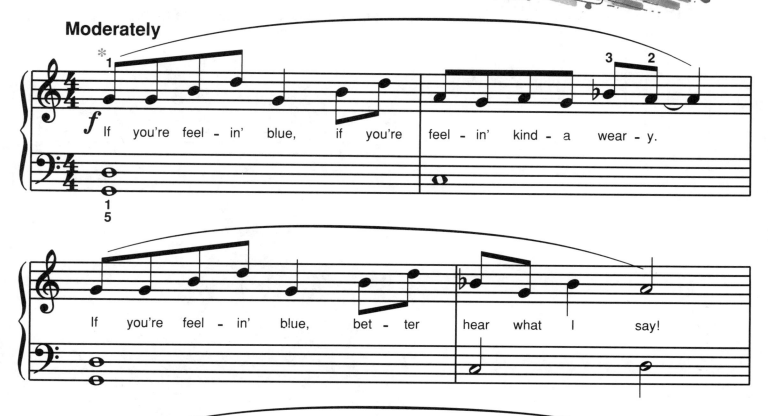

**Moderately**

If you're feel - in' blue, if you're feel - in' kind - a wear - y.

If you're feel - in' blue, bet - ter hear what I say!

Play this rock - in' tune, it will sure - ly make you cheer - ry;

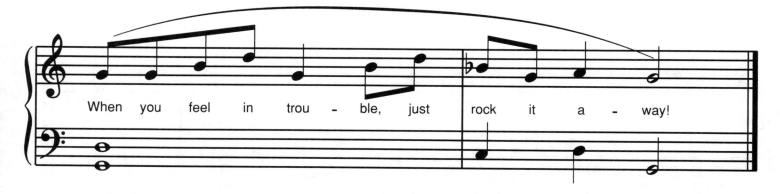

When you feel in trou - ble, just rock it a - way!

*OPTIONAL: Pairs of eighth notes may be played long    short, long    short, etc.

# G Position with LH an Octave Higher

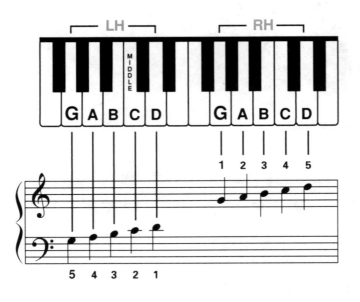

In this NEW G POSITION, the LEFT hand plays ONE OCTAVE HIGHER than before. The RIGHT HAND remains in the same position.

There is only ONE new LH note to learn.

*NEW NOTE*

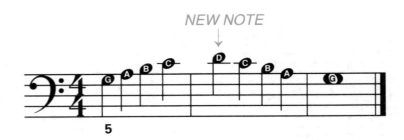

## New Position G

**Moderately**

```
1. "G      G      G   A   B,      B   A   B   C      D,
2.  G,     G,     Gee what fun,   play-ing up  to    D!
```

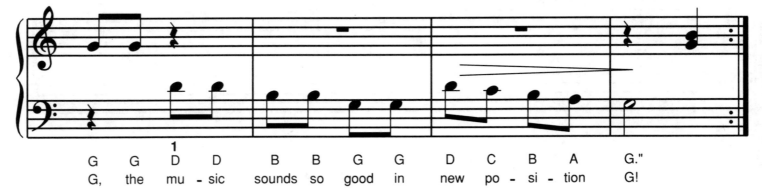

```
G   G   D   D      B   B   G   G      D   C   B   A      G."
G,  the mu - sic   sounds so  good in new po - si - tion G!
```

# Can't Get 'Em Up!

**Moderately fast**

Military bugle call

*f* We can't get 'em up, we can't get 'em up, we can't get 'em up this morn - ing! We

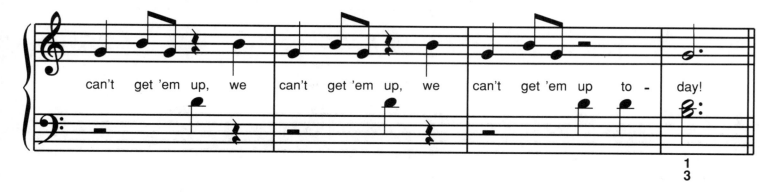

can't get 'em up, we can't get 'em up, we can't get 'em up to - day!

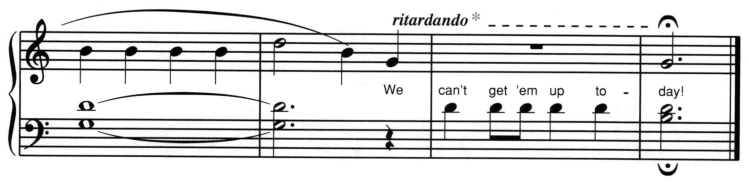

We can't get 'em up to - day!

*ritardando* *_____*

\* **ritardando** means *gradually slowing.*

# I've Been Wishin'

**Happily**

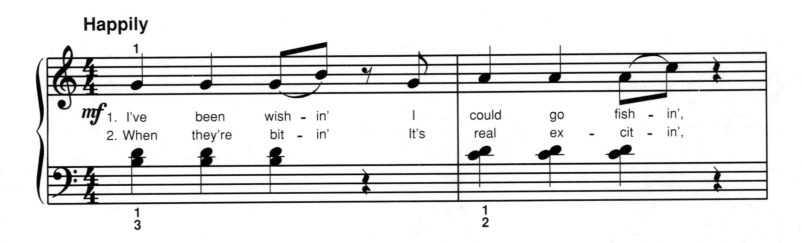

1. I've been wish - in' I could go fish - in',
2. When they're bit - in' It's real ex - cit - in',

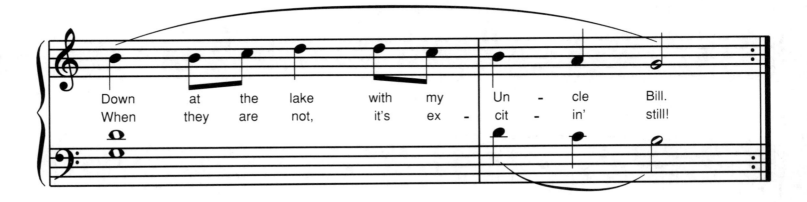

Down at the lake with my Un - cle Bill.
When they are not, it's ex - cit - in' still!

**DUET PART** (Student plays 1 octave higher.)

*D.C. al Fine*

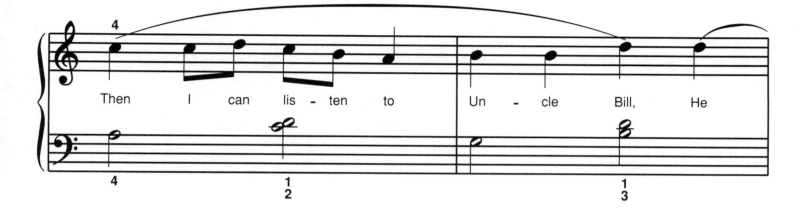

Then I can lis - ten to Un - cle Bill, He

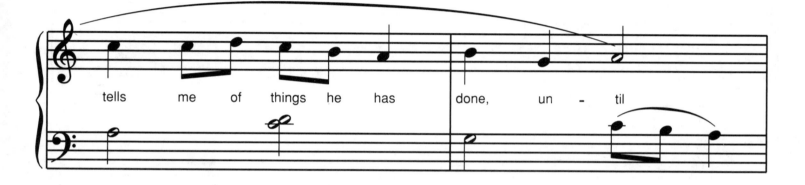

tells me of things he has done, un - til

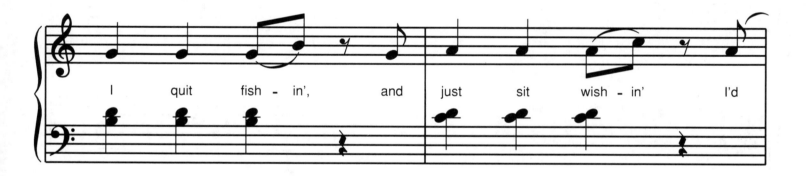

I quit fish - in', and just sit wish - in' I'd

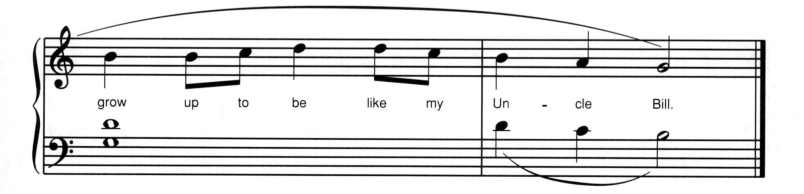

grow up to be like my Un - cle Bill.

# Für Ludwig*

**Not too fast, but with great optimism**

*Move LH*
*to Low G Position*

**5**

*Ludwig van Beethoven—composer of Für Elise (For Elise).*

Music does not always stay in ONE KEYBOARD POSITION. This piece uses C POSITION and NEW G POSITION, then moves up and down to different octaves. As you make use of more range over the keyboard, your playing becomes more fun and more interesting to listen to.

# Amigos

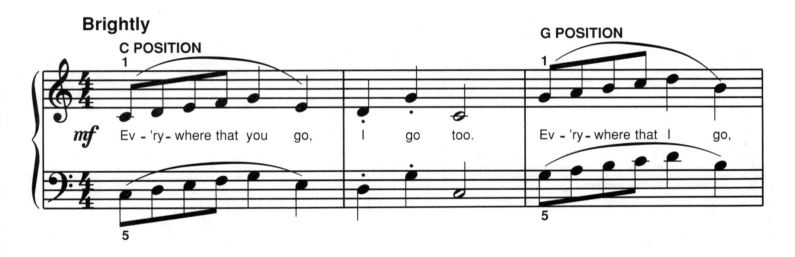

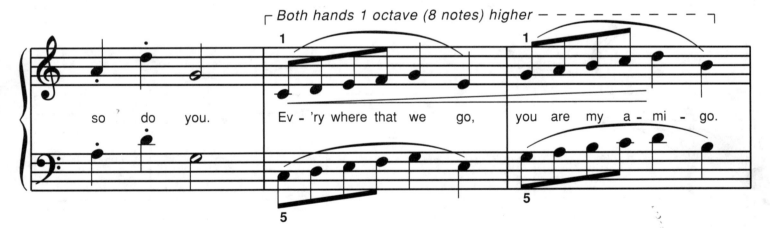

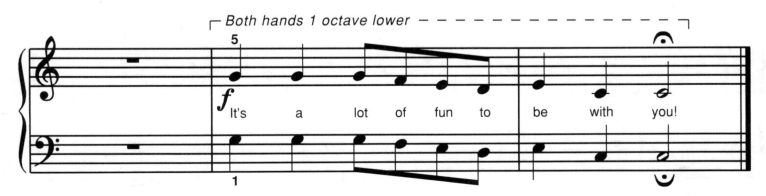

You are now ready to begin Prep SACRED SOLOS, Level D.

*8va* ⌐ placed OVER the staff means *play the notes 1 octave HIGHER than written.*

*8va* ⌐ placed UNDER the staff means *play the notes 1 octave LOWER than written.*

# My Computer

**Moderately fast**

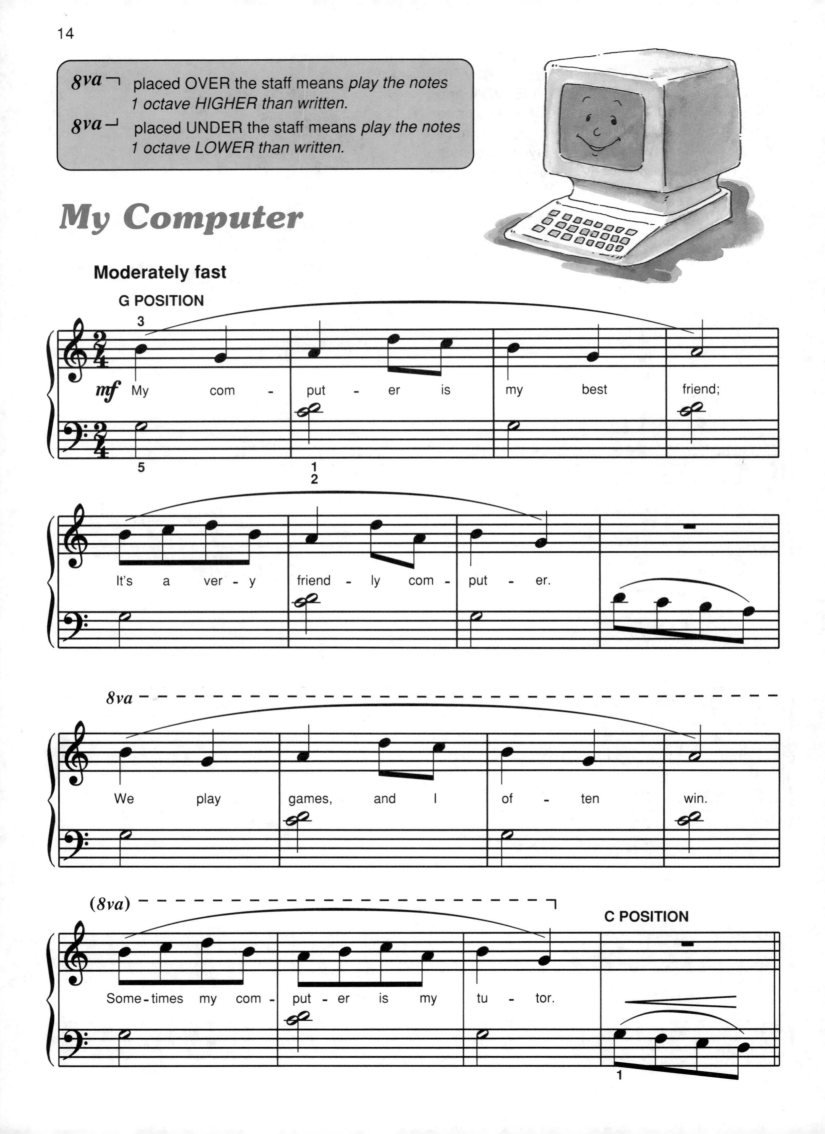

It can teach me to play a song;

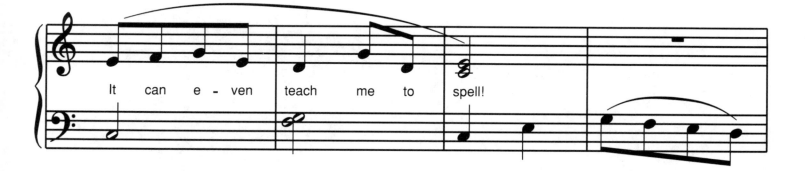

It can e - ven teach me to spell!

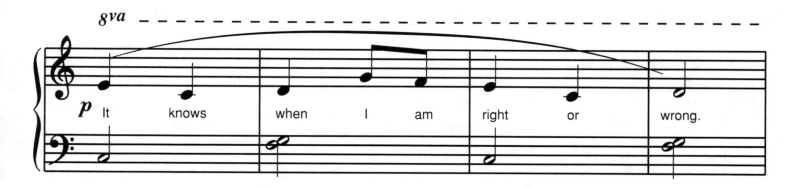

It knows when I am right or wrong.

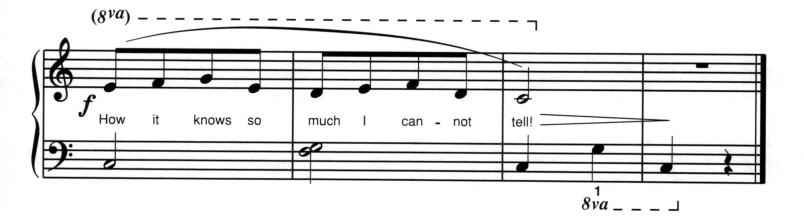

How it knows so much I can - not tell!

# Tempo Marks

**TEMPO** is an Italian word.  It means "RATE OF SPEED."

Words indicating the rate of speed used in playing music
are called **TEMPO MARKS.**

Here are some of the most important tempo marks:

| | | |
|---|---|---|
| **ADAGIO** | = | Slowly. |
| **ANDANTE** | = | Moving along.  The word actually means "walking." |
| **MODERATO** | = | Moderately. |
| **ALLEGRO** | = | Quickly, happily. |

These words may be combined.  For example:

**ALLEGRO MODERATO** = Moderately fast.

# Minuet and Trio
## in Classical Style

**G POSITION**

**Minuet**

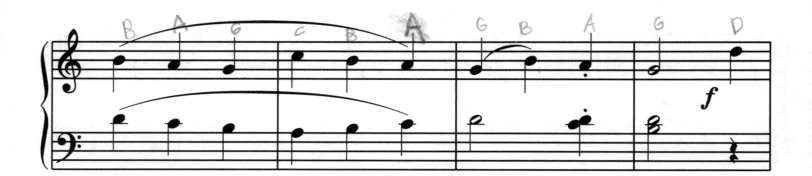

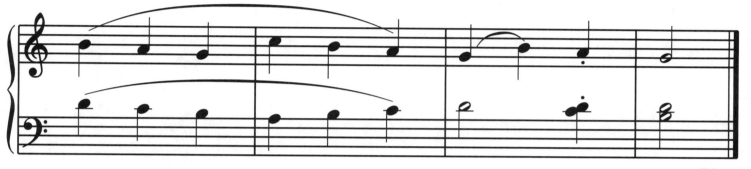

*Fine*

## Trio

**C POSITION**   *sept 9*

*2nd time, play both hands 8va*

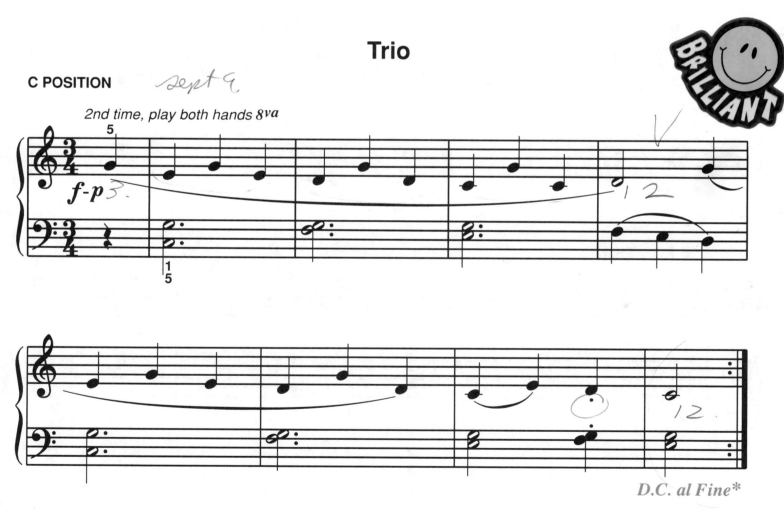

*D.C. al Fine\**

(After repeating the TRIO *8va*,
play the MINUET again, ending at the Fine.)

*\*D.C. al Fine (Da Capo al Fine)* means repeat from the beginning and play to the end *(Fine)*.

18

# Filling in the Positions
# Going UP the Keyboard

You will now find it easy to play in every white key position between C POSITION and G POSITION. In *FOUR POSITION MARCH,* after playing the first 2 measures, just move the 5 fingers of each hand one key to the right for each position change.

The pattern of the first 2 measures is repeated in D POSITION, then again in E POSITION.

In F POSITION, only the last 4 notes of the pattern are different.

# Four Position March

**Andante**

*Sept. 9*

*2nd time, play both hands 8va*

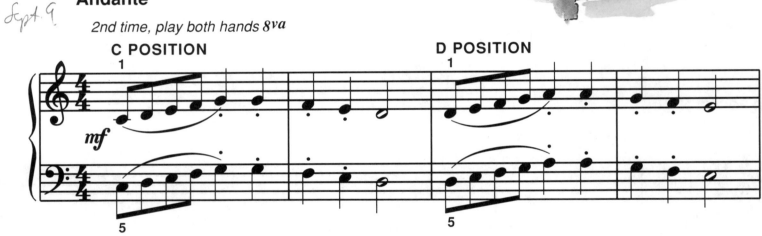

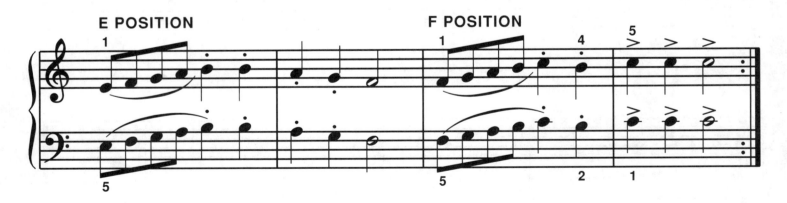

**DUET PART** (Student plays 1 octave higher 1st time, 2 octaves higher 2nd time.)

# Filling in the Positions
# Going DOWN the Keyboard

After you place the correct finger on the starting note of each position, it is easy to play by reading INTERVALS in each pattern.

In *FIVE POSITION WALTZ,* the patterns move down in 2nds and up in 3rds.

REMEMBER: Each 5 finger position is named for the LOWEST note in each position, played with RH 1 or LH 5.

## *Five Position Waltz*

Sept. 16

**Moderato**

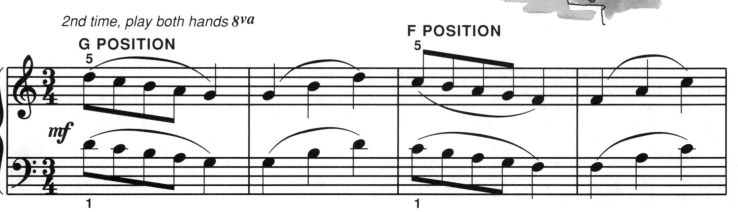

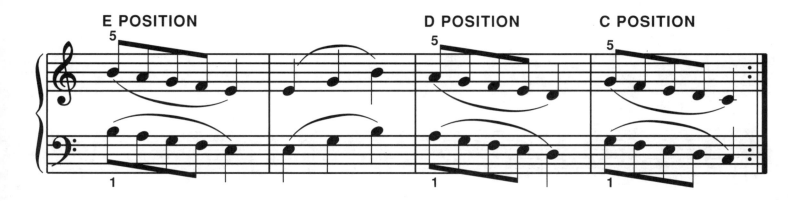

**DUET PART** (Student plays 1 octave higher 1st time, 2 octaves higher 2nd time.)

# Blue and Low

*Sept 16*

**Andante**

*Optional: Play both hands 1 octave lower throughout this piece.*

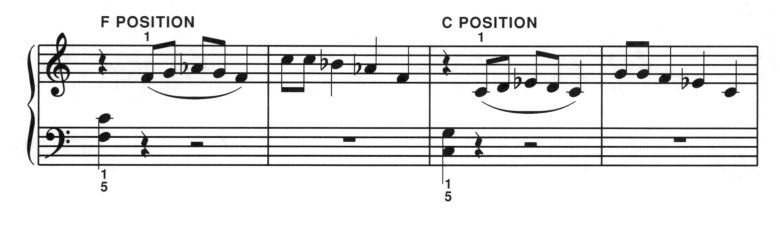

*OPTIONAL: Pairs of eighth notes may be played long   short, long   short, *etc.*

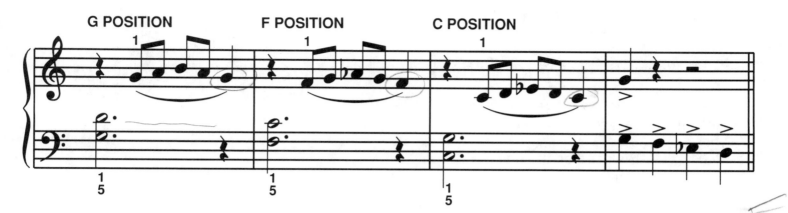

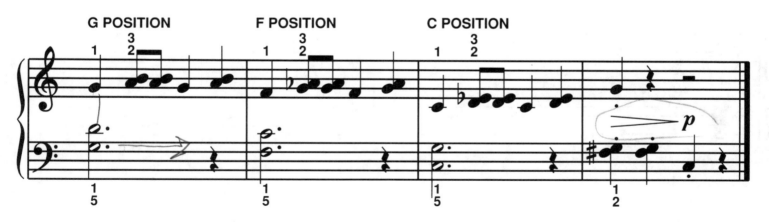

*OPTIONAL: Each time this rhythm ( ♩ ♫ ♩ ♩ ) appears, you may use the following rhythm for a more interesting sound:

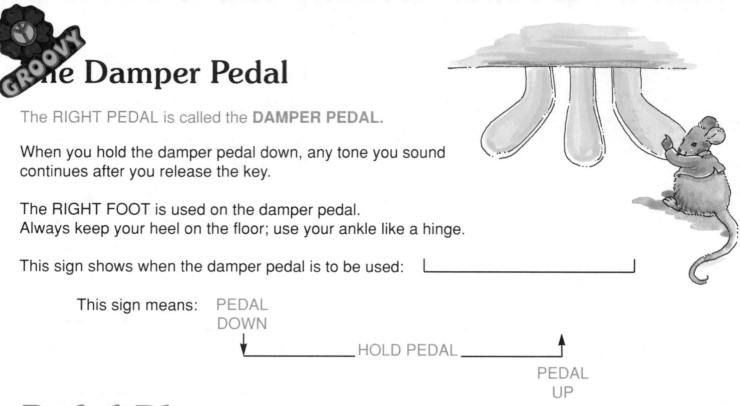

# The Damper Pedal

The RIGHT PEDAL is called the **DAMPER PEDAL.**

When you hold the damper pedal down, any tone you sound continues after you release the key.

The RIGHT FOOT is used on the damper pedal.
Always keep your heel on the floor; use your ankle like a hinge.

This sign shows when the damper pedal is to be used:

This sign means:    PEDAL
DOWN

HOLD PEDAL

PEDAL
UP

# Pedal Play

This easy PEDAL STUDY will show you how the damper pedal causes the tones to continue to sound, EVEN AFTER YOUR HANDS HAVE RELEASED THE KEYS.

Press the pedal down as you play each group of notes.  Hold it down through the rests.

Notice that the HAND POSITION CHANGES FOR EACH GROUP OF NOTES!

Play **VERY SLOWLY** and **LISTEN.**

**Adagio**

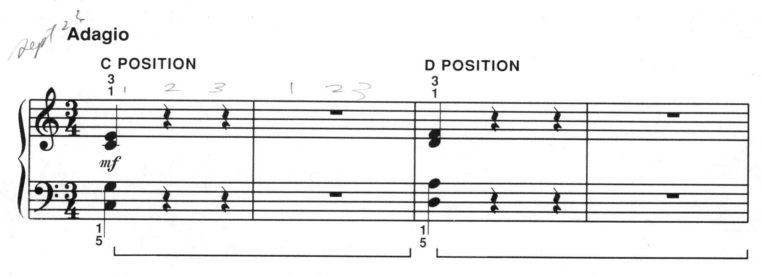

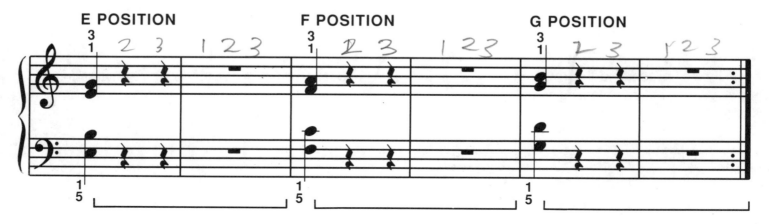

# *Harp Song*

**IMPORTANT!** Notice that the HAND POSITION changes every 2 measures!

**Moderato**

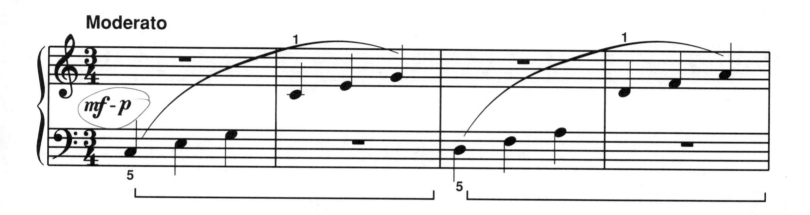

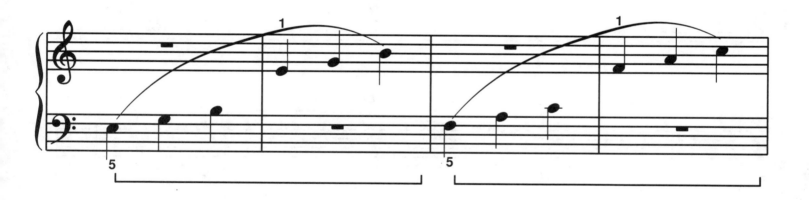

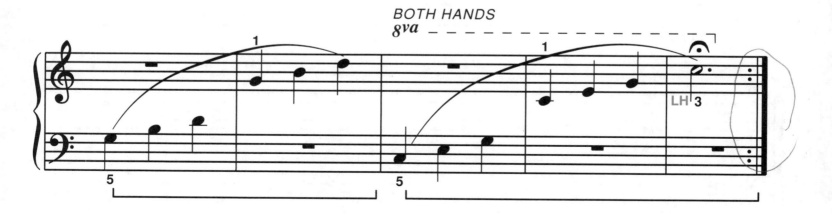

24

# A Concert Piece

**Moderato**

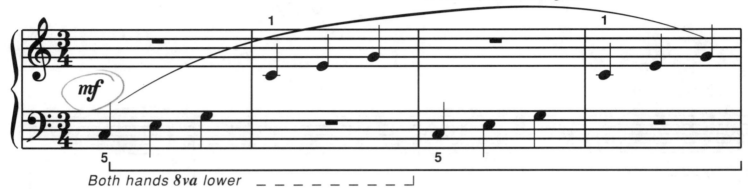

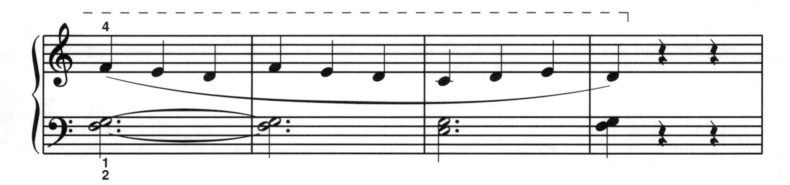

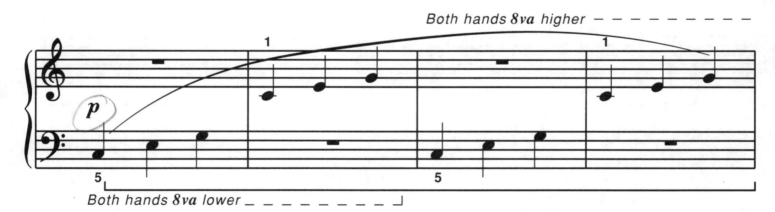

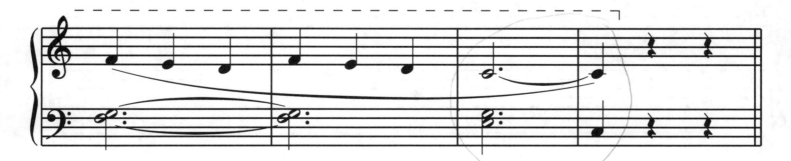

*Both hands 8va higher* — — — — — — — — —

*f*

*Both hands 8va lower* — — — — — — — — ⌐

(✱) Don't start too low

*Both hands 8va higher* — — — — — — — — —

*p*

*Both hands 8va lower* — — — — — — — — ⌐

## CODA (an added ending)

*Play as written*

4

*p* —————————————— *f* >

1
2

*8va*

# Measuring Half Steps or Semi tone

A **HALF STEP** is the distance from any key to the very next key above or below, whether black or white.

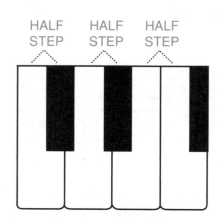

**HALF STEPS • NO KEY BETWEEN**

The SHARP sign ♯ raises a note a half step (play next key to the right).

The FLAT sign ♭ lowers a note a half step (play next key to the left).

Each black key may be named 2 ways:

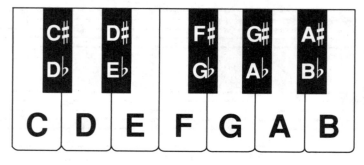

The NATURAL sign ♮ cancels a sharp or flat!

A note after a natural sign is ALWAYS A WHITE KEY!

The following measures contain only notes that are a HALF STEP apart.
Play with hands separate. Say the note names as you play: "B, A sharp, B," etc.

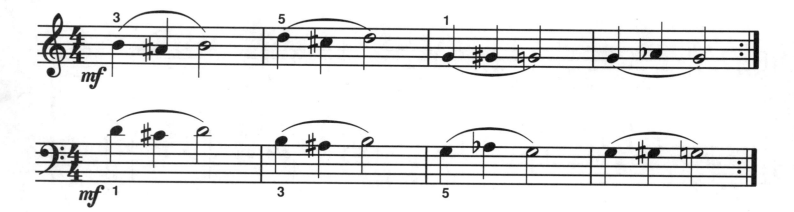

# Rockin' Half Steps

**Allegro moderato**

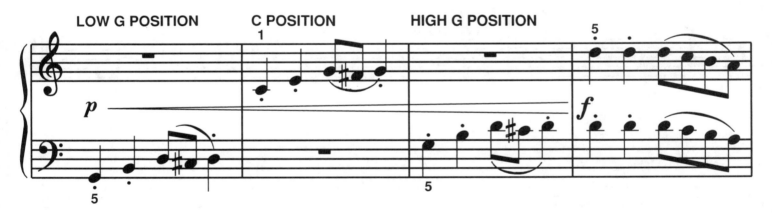

*Play the last line 3 times: 1st time ***f***, 2nd time ***mf***, 3rd time ***p***.

# Boogie-Woogie Goose

**Allegro moderato**

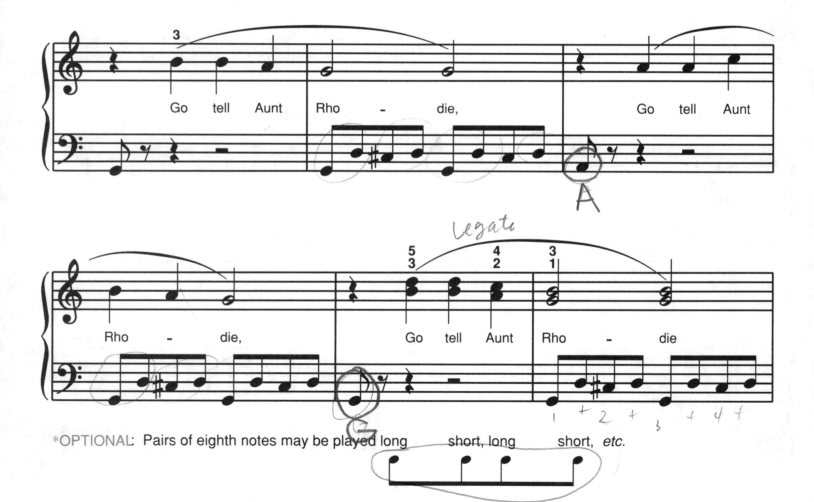

*OPTIONAL: Pairs of eighth notes may be played long    short, long    short, *etc.*

her goose is - n't dead.

It's do-in' the boo - gie, It's do-in' the

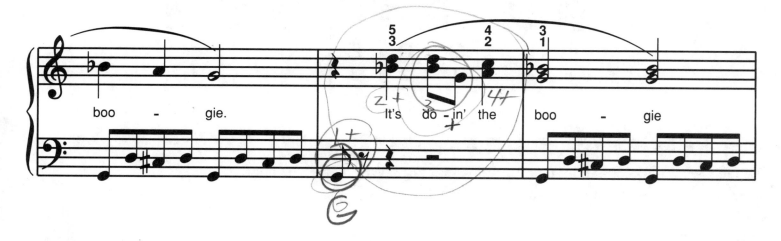

boo - gie. It's do-in' the boo - gie

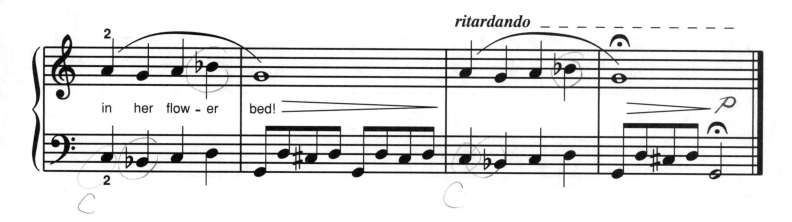

*ritardando*

in her flow - er bed!

# Measuring Whole Steps

A **WHOLE STEP** is equal to 2 half steps.
Skip one key . . . black or white.

**WHOLE STEPS · ONE KEY BETWEEN**

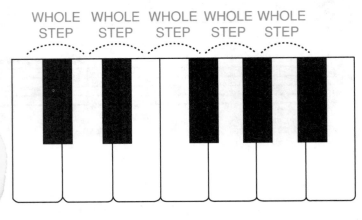

The following keys are used in *THE PLANETS:*

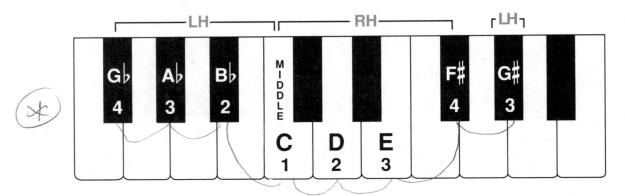

## Preparation for *THE PLANETS*

The following measures contain only notes that are a WHOLE STEP apart.
Play with hands separate, several times.  Say the note names as you play.

**MIDDLE C POSITION**

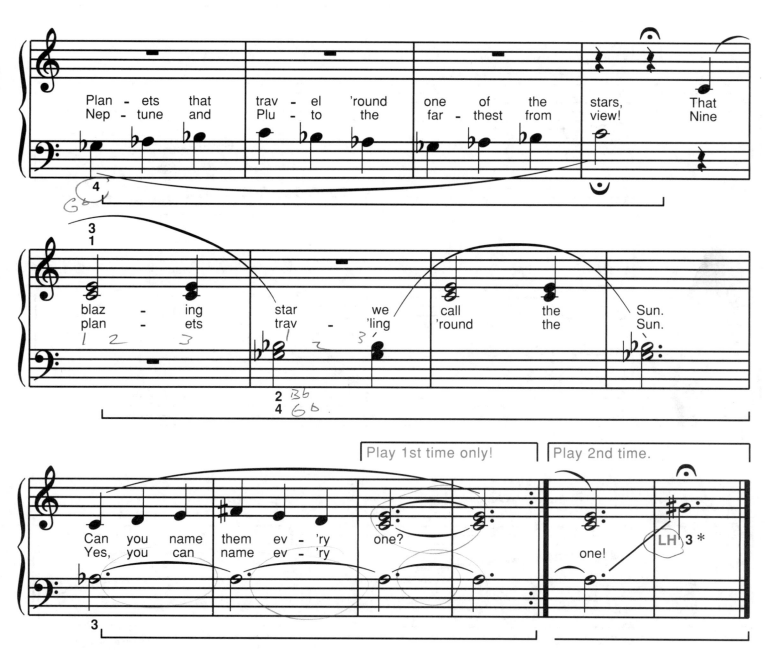

# The Planets

Dec 2.

**Andante**

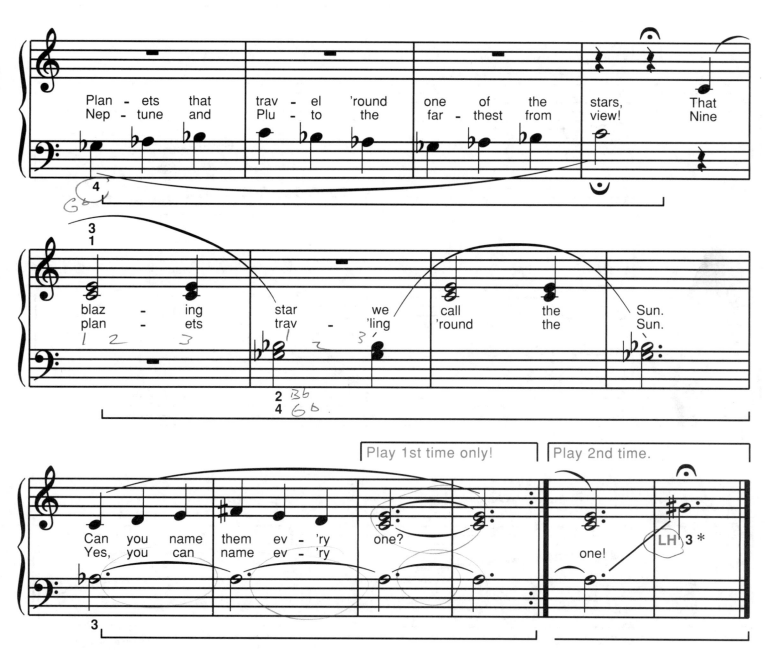

1. Mer - cu - ry, Ve - nus, and Earth, and then Mars;
2. Ju - pi - ter, Sat - urn, and U - ra - nus, too;

Plan - ets that trav - el 'round one of the stars, That
Nep - tune and Plu - to 'round the far - thest from view! Nine

blaz - ing star we call the Sun.
plan - ets trav - 'ling 'round the Sun.

Play 1st time only!
Can you name them ev - 'ry one?
Yes, you can name ev - 'ry

Play 2nd time.
one!

*Optional: Play the last note of the piece $8^{va}$.

# What a Happy Day!

**Allegro moderato**

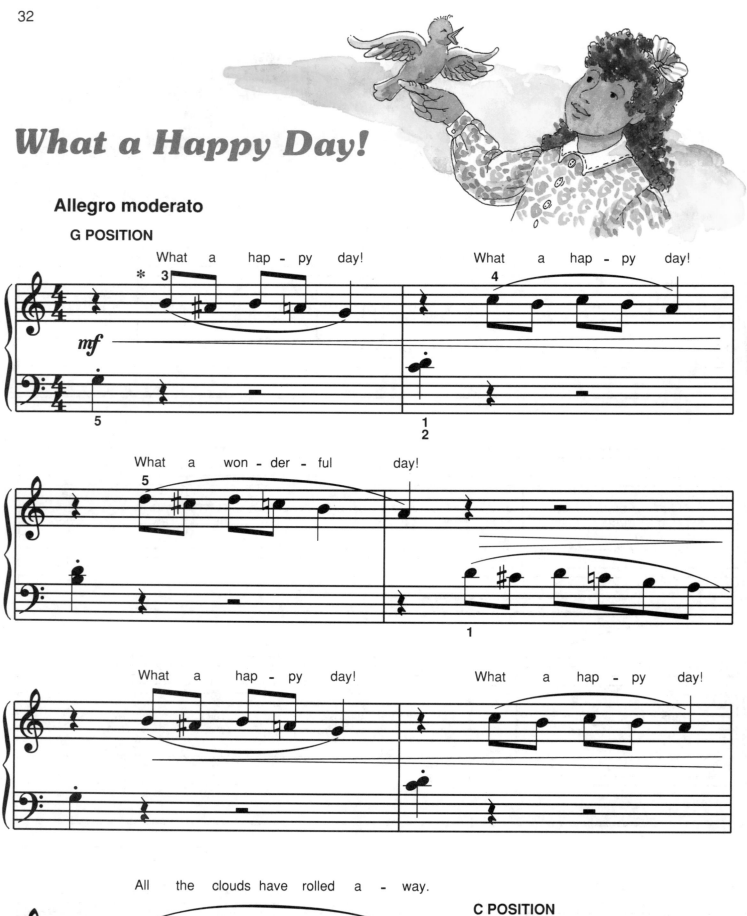

*Pairs of eighth notes may be played a bit unevenly.

# The Thing that Has No Name!

**Mysteriously**

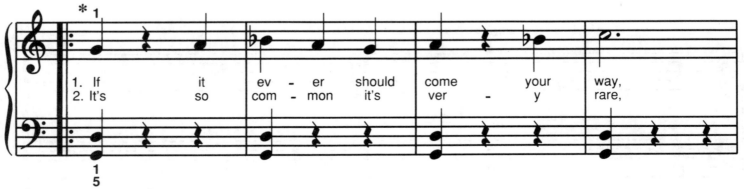

1. If it ev - er should come your way,
2. It's so com - mon it's ver - y rare,

*Optional: Play RH *8va* lower.

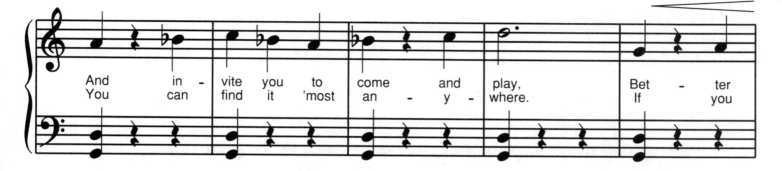

And in - vite you to come and play, Bet - ter
You can find it 'most an - y - where. If you

hur - ry and run a - way from the thing
see it you'd best be - ware of the thing

that has no name!
that has no name!

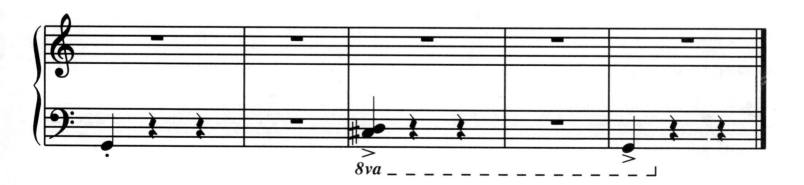

# Tetrachords

A TETRACHORD is a series of FOUR NOTES having a pattern of

## WHOLE STEP, WHOLE STEP, HALF STEP

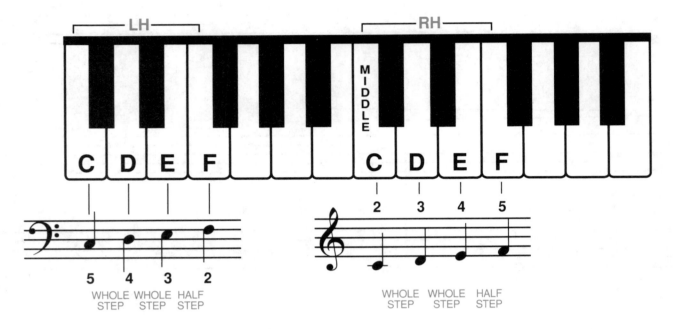

The notes of a TETRACHORD are always in ALPHABETICAL order,
and must have this pattern:  WHOLE STEP,  WHOLE STEP,  HALF STEP.

PLAY THE FOLLOWING TETRACHORDS.

**LH** tetrachords are fingered **5 4 3 2**.

**RH** tetrachords are fingered **2 3 4 5**.

### C TETRACHORDS

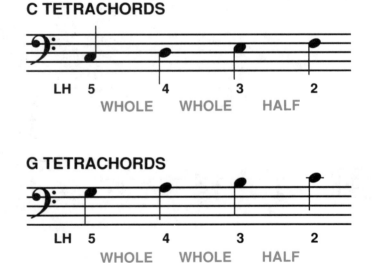

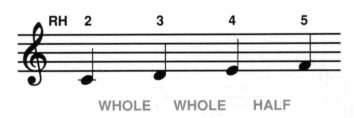

### G TETRACHORDS

### D TETRACHORDS

# The Major Scale

The MAJOR SCALE is made of **TWO TETRACHORDS** *joined* by a **WHOLE STEP**.

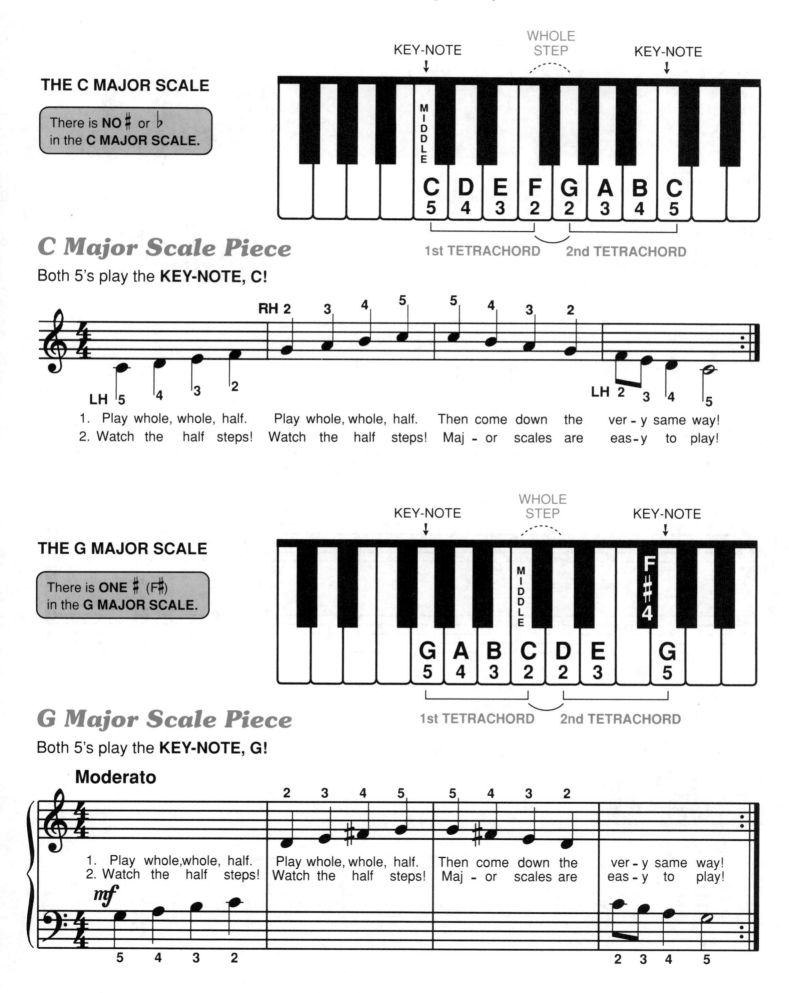

**THE C MAJOR SCALE**

There is **NO** ♯ or ♭ in the **C MAJOR SCALE**.

## C Major Scale Piece

Both 5's play the **KEY-NOTE, C!**

1. Play whole, whole, half.   Play whole, whole, half.   Then come down the   ver - y same way!
2. Watch the half steps!   Watch the half steps!   Maj - or scales are   eas - y to play!

**THE G MAJOR SCALE**

There is **ONE** ♯ (F♯) in the **G MAJOR SCALE**.

## G Major Scale Piece

Both 5's play the **KEY-NOTE, G!**

**Moderato**

1. Play whole, whole, half.   Play whole, whole, half.   Then come down the   ver - y same way!
2. Watch the half steps!   Watch the half steps!   Maj - or scales are   eas - y to play!

# The Key of G Major

A piece based on the G major scale is in the KEY OF G MAJOR.
Since F is sharp in the G scale, every F is sharp.

Instead of placing a sharp before every F,
the sharp is indicated at the beginning in the KEY SIGNATURE.

## *Carol* in *G Major*

**HAND POSITION:** RH plays the upper tetrachord,
LH plays the lower tetrachord.

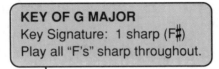

**KEY OF G MAJOR**
Key Signature: 1 sharp (F♯)
Play all "F's" sharp throughout.

**Moderato**

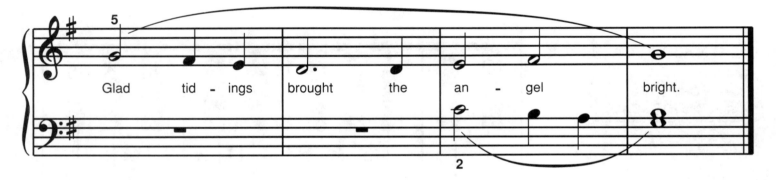

*mf* While by my sheep I watched at night,

Glad tid - ings brought the an - gel bright.

## *The Same Carol in C Major*

**HAND POSITION:** RH plays the upper tetrachord, LH plays the lower tetrachord.

**KEY OF C MAJOR**
Key Signature: no ♯, no ♭.

**Moderato**

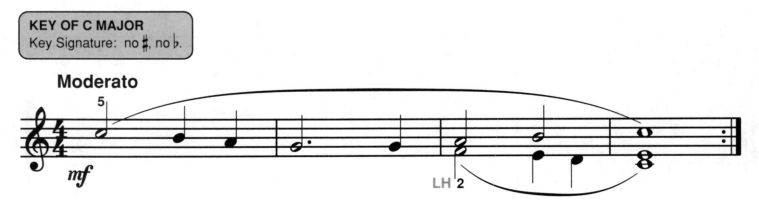

*mf*

# Three Wise Monkeys

**KEY OF G MAJOR**
Key Signature: 1 sharp (F♯)
Play all "F's" sharp throughout.

**HAND POSITION:** LH plays the lower tetrachord.
RH plays the upper tetrachord.

**Allegro moderato**

*mf* Three wise mon - keys in a tree; One won't lis - ten, one won't see.

One won't speak to you or me; Three wise mon - keys in a tree.

*f* Please, lit - tle mon - keys, WISE UP!

FOR MORE FUN: Play also in C TETRACHORD POSITION (5's on C's one octave apart).

# The Mermaid

**HAND POSITION:** LH plays the lower tetrachord. RH plays the upper tetrachord.

**KEY OF G MAJOR**
Key Signature: 1 sharp (F#)
Play all "F's" sharp throughout.

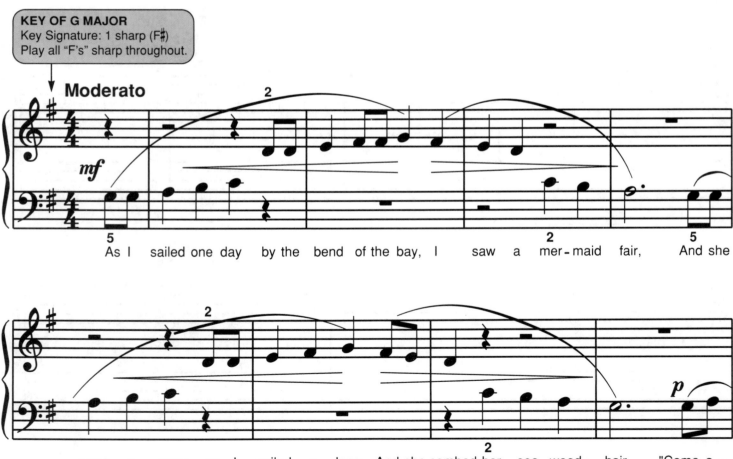

As I sailed one day by the bend of the bay, I saw a mer-maid fair, And she

sang a song as I sailed a-long, And she combed her sea-weed hair, "Come a-

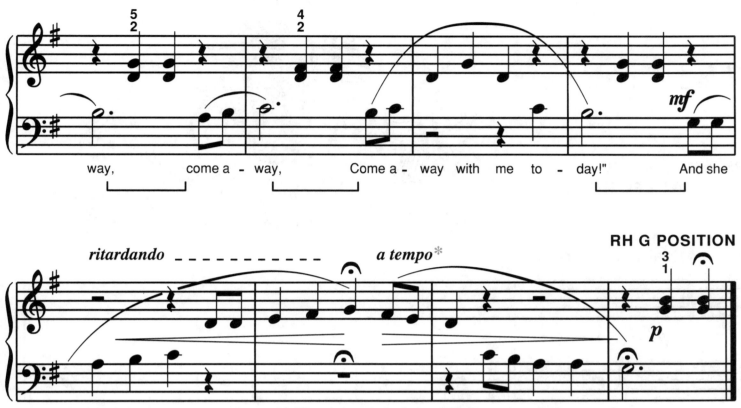

way, come a - way, Come a - way with me to - day!" And she

**RH G POSITION**

winked her eye as I said, "Good-bye," And she waved as I sailed a - way.

*a tempo means resume original speed.*

**DUET PART** (Student plays 1 octave lower.)

# The Caravan

**RH in C POSITION**
**LH in LOW G POSITION**

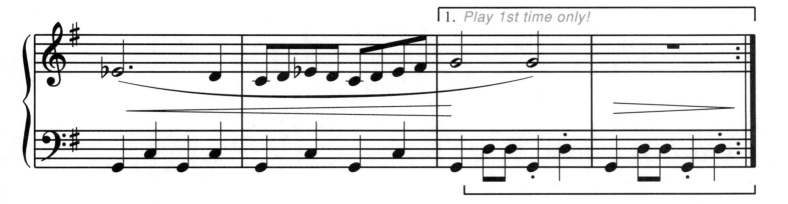

1. *Play 1st time only!*

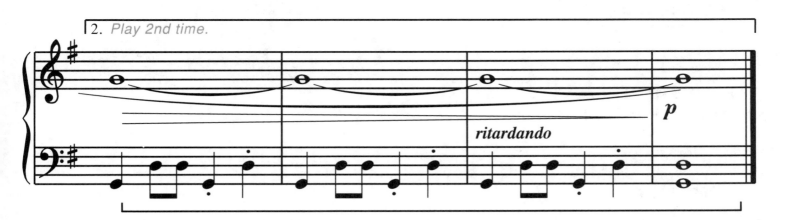

2. *Play 2nd time.*

ritardando

*p*

**DUET PART** (Student plays as written.)

Play DUET PART **8va** 2nd time.

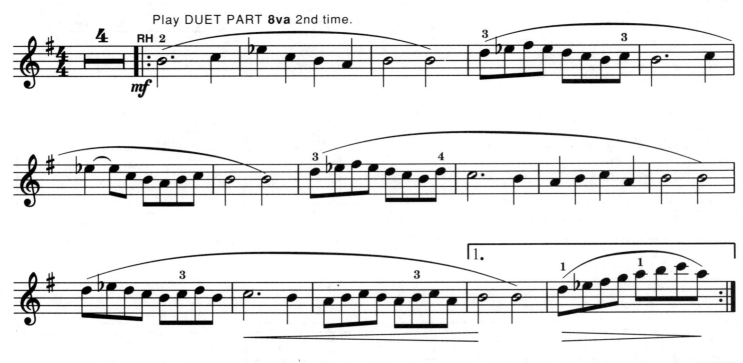

ritardando

*p*

# The Baseball Game

**RH in C POSITION**
**LH in LOW G POSITION**

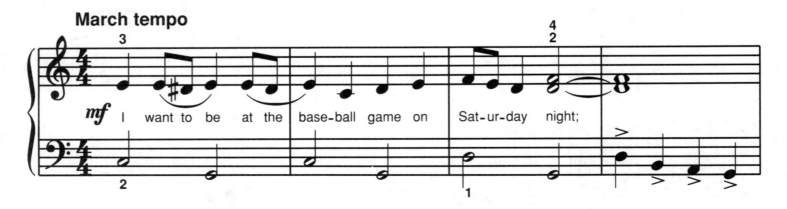

I want to be at the base-ball game on Sat-ur-day night;

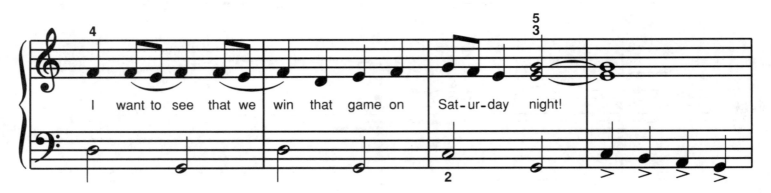

I want to see that we win that game on Sat-ur-day night!

I want to hear when the um-pire says "Strike one, strike two, strike three!"

45

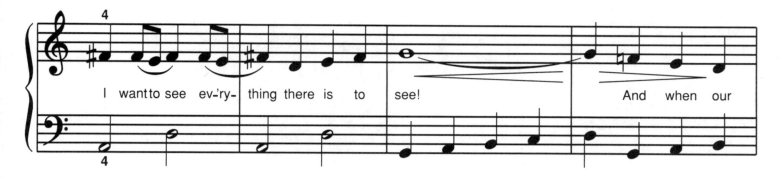

I want to see ev-'ry- thing there is to see! And when our

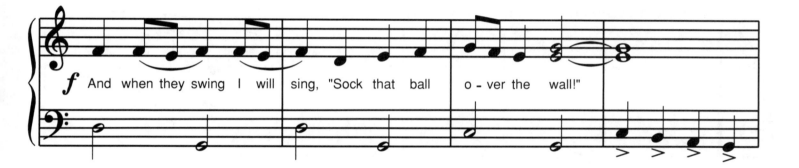

team comes to bat I will jump and yell and hol-ler and call,

*f* And when they swing I will sing, "Sock that ball o - ver the wall!"

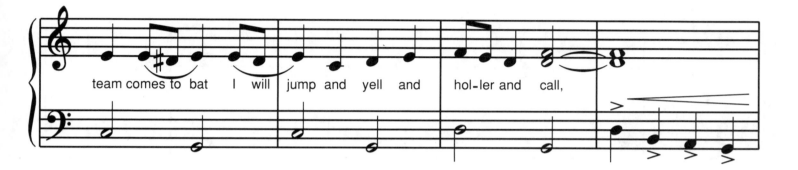

Watch - ing a game is a lot of fun when our play - ers knock out a big home run, and

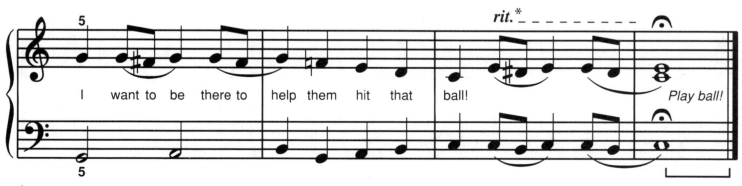

*rit.* _____ 

I want to be there to help them hit that ball! Play ball!

*rit.* or *ritard.*—abbreviation for *ritardando*

# Ta-dah!

**RH in C POSITION**
**LH in LOW G POSITION**

**Allegro**

*Both hands 8va* _ _ _ _ _ _ _ _ _ _ _ _ _ _ _

*f* Ta - dah!   Ta - dah! Ta - dah! Ta - dah!

**With great pomp and power, not too slow!**   *(RH as written)*

Boom!   Boom!   Boom!   Boom!   1. Sound the trum - pets,
2. See how proud the

*LH one octave lower*

here I come!   Ring the bells and   rat - tle the drum!
peo - ple look!   Shake my hand, I   fin - ished the book!

*Both hands 8va* _ _ _ _ _ _ _ _ _ _ _ _ _ _ _ _ _ _ _ _ _

*ritard.* _ _ _ _ _ _ _ _ _ _ _ _ _ _ _

Ta - dah!   Ta - dah! Ta - dah! Ta - dah!

# Review of Musical Terms

| | |
|---|---|
| Accent (>) | placed over or under a note that gets special emphasis. Play the note louder. |
| Accidental | a sharp or flat not given in the key signature. |
| Adagio | slowly. |
| Allegro | quickly, happily. |
| Andante | moving along (at walking speed). |
| *a tempo* | resume original speed. |
| *crescendo* ( ◁══ ) | gradually louder. |
| Da Capo al Fine (**D. C. al Fine**) | repeat from the beginning and play to the **Fine** (end). |
| *diminuendo* ( ══▷ ) | gradually softer. |
| Dynamic signs | signs showing how loud or soft to play. |
| Fermata (⌢) | indicates that a note should be held longer than its true value. |
| *Fine* | the end. |
| First ending (⌐1. ⌐) | the measures under the bracket are played the first time only. |
| Flat sign (♭) | lowers a note one half step. Play the next key to the left. |
| Forte (*f*) | loud. |
| Half step | the distance from one key to the very next one, with no key between. |
| Harmonic interval | the interval between two tones sounded together. |
| Incomplete measure | a measure at the beginning of a piece with fewer counts than shown in the time signature. The missing counts are found in the last measure. |
| Interval | the difference in pitch (highness or lowness) between two tones. |
| Key signature | the number of sharps or flats in any key—written at the beginning of each line. |
| Legato | smoothly connected. Usually indicated by a slur over or under the notes. |
| Major scale | a series of eight notes made of two tetrachords joined by a whole step. |
| Melodic interval | the interval between two tones sounded separately. |
| Mezzo forte (*mf*) | moderately loud. |
| Moderato | moderately. |
| Natural sign (♮) | cancels a sharp or flat. |
| Octave sign (*8va*) | when placed OVER notes, means play them one octave higher; when placed UNDER notes, means play them one octave lower. |
| Pedal mark ( ⌐____⌐ ) | press the damper pedal, hold it, and release it. |
| Piano (*p*) | soft. |
| Repeat signs ‖ | repeat from the beginning. |
| ‖ ‖ | repeat the measures between the double bars. |
| *ritardando* (abbreviated **ritard.** or **rit.**) | gradually slowing. |
| Second ending (⌐2. ⌐) | the measures under the bracket are played the second time only. |
| Sharp sign (♯) | raises a note one half step. Play the next key to the right. |
| Staccato | separated or detached. Usually indicated by a dot over or under the note. |
| Tempo | rate of speed. |
| Tetrachord | four notes in alphabetical order, having the pattern of WHOLE STEP, WHOLE STEP, HALF STEP. |
| Time signatures ($\frac{2}{4}$, $\frac{3}{4}$, $\frac{4}{4}$) | numbers found at the beginning of a piece or section of a piece. The top number shows the number of beats in each measure. The bottom number shows the kind of note that gets one beat. |
| Whole step | two half steps. The distance between two keys with one key between. |

# Certificate of Promotion

## This Certifies that

_____

has successfully completed
**Prep Course Level D**
and is hereby promoted to
**Prep Course Level E**
or **Alfred's Basic Course Level 2.**

ALFRED'S BASICS PIANO LIBRARY

_____
Date

_____
Teacher